Object Lessons
Using Children's Toys

Object Lessons Series

Bess, C. W., *Children's Object Sermons for the Seasons,* 1026-8

Bess, C. W., *Object-Centered Children's Sermons,* 0734-8

Bess, C. W., *Sparkling Object Sermons for Children,* 0824-7

Bess, C. W., & Roy DeBrand, *Bible-Centered Object Sermons for Children,* 0886-7

Biller, Tom & Martie, *Simple Object Lessons for Children,* 0793-3

Bruinsma, Sheryl, *Easy-to-Use Object Lessons,* 0832-8

Bruinsma, Sheryl, *More Object Lessons for Very Young Children,* 1075-6

Bruinsma, Sheryl, *New Object Lessons,* 0775-5

Bruinsma, Sheryl, *Object Lessons for Every Occasion,* 0994-4

Bruinsma, Sheryl, *Object Lessons for Special Days,* 0920-0

Bruinsma, Sheryl, *Object Lessons for Very Young Children,* 0956-1

Claassen, David, *Object Lessons for a Year,* 2514-1

Connelly, H. W., *47 Object Lessons for Youth Programs,* 2314-9

Coombs, Robert, *Concise Object Sermons for Children,* 2541-9

Coombs, Robert, *Enlightening Object Lessons for Children,* 2567-2

Cooper, Charlotte, *50 Object Stories for Children,* 2523-0

Cross, Luther, *Easy Object Stories,* 2502-8

Cross, Luther, *Object Lessons for Children,* 2315-7

Cross, Luther, *Story Sermons for Children,* 2328-9

De Jonge, Joanne, *More Object Lessons from Nature,* 3004-8

De Jonge, Joanne, *Object Lessons from Nature,* 2989-9

De Jonge, Joanne, *Object Lessons from Pebbles and Paper Clips,* 5041-3

De Jonge, Joanne, *Object Lessons from Your Home and Yard,* 3026-9

Edstrom, Lois, *Contemporary Object Lessons for Children's Church,* 3432-9

Gebhardt, Richard, & Mark Armstrong, *Object Lessons from Science Experiments,* 3811-1

Godsey, Kyle, *Object Lessons About God,* 3841-3

Hendricks, William, *Object Lessons Based on Bible Characters,* 4373-5

Hendricks, William, & Merle Den Bleyker, *Object Lessons from Sports and Games,* 4134-1

Hendricks, William, & Merle Den Bleyker, *Object Lessons That Teach Bible Truths,* 4172-4

Loeks, Mary, *Object Lessons for Children's Worship,* 5584-9

McDonald, Roderick, *Successful Object Sermons,* 6270-5

Runk, Wesley, *Object Lessons from the Bible,* 7698-6

Squyres, Greg, *Simple Object Lessons for Young Children,* 8330-3

Sullivan, Jessie, *Object Lessons and Stories for Children's Church,* 8037-1

Sullivan, Jessie, *Object Lessons with Easy-to-Find Objects,* 8190-4

Trull, Joe, *40 Object Sermons for Children,* 8831-3

Object Lessons
Using Children's Toys

Sheryl Bruinsma

Baker Books

A Division of Baker Book House Co
Grand Rapids, Michigan 49516

To Hailey Nicole Bruinsma,
our newest grandchild

©1996 by Sheryl Bruinsma

Published by Baker Books
a division of Baker Book House Company
P.O. Box 6287, Grand Rapids, MI 49516-6287

ISBN 0-8010-5695-0

Printed in the United States of America

Contents

* These eight lessons use the items in the Fisher-Price child's medical kit. Any toy doctor or nurse kit will contain most, if not all, of the items. Using the items from one source makes a convenient series.

Christian Living

Current Issues

Using Object Lessons to Teach

Like the biblical parables, object lessons are an effective way to teach spiritual truths. This is especially true for children because the object, in addition to holding a child's attention, gives the child a familiar frame of reference to help him or her understand an abstract concept.

This book is centered around the most familiar of all objects to children—their toys. The toys used in the following object lessons are found in most households with children, and you should be able to obtain them easily. The children themselves could even take turns bringing in a toy for you to use.

Each lesson contains an outline that gives an overview of the concept to be presented. This should help you find the lesson to fit your particular need. Introductory and concluding remarks are included in the outline to help you begin and end the lesson smoothly. The lesson is given just as I would present it, but change it to fit your style.

When giving an object lesson to children, be enthusiastic. Enthusiasm is contagious, and you want children to enjoy spiritual truths. Use an engaging tone of voice to hold their attention. Remember to stick to your point and not get carried away with the object. Adjust your vocabulary to the age of the children. If you use language they don't understand, they will not understand the truth you are teaching. And remember, the toys should cooperate for you, but children are always unpredictable. For a more complete guide on how to give object lessons, see my first book, *New Object Lessons*.

The lessons in this book are also written so that they may be read to children. I hope you will use them for family devotions as well as for church or school groups.

1

A New Season

Object: a football (any size)

Lesson: A Christian group works together as a team.

Outline

Introduce object: What kind of a ball is this?

1. Football is a group game. We are a group.
2. The purpose of a football team is to win the game. The purpose of our group is to have winning Christian lives.
3. Everyone on the team needs to work together.

Conclusion: Will you all be good team members?

What kind of ball is this? Yes, it is a football. How many of you have a football? It is probably the only ball we use that is not round.

Did you ever see anyone try to play football alone? Can you imagine anyone throwing a pass and then chasing it? I wonder what it would be like kicking the football and trying to run to catch it. Football is meant to be played by a group of people.

This is a new season for us. We are here as a group. We are here because we want to be together. We want to work together. We want to learn together. It wouldn't be much fun if only one person came. We need our whole group for our activities.

The purpose of a football team is to score the most points and win the game. Our group has a purpose too.

It is to learn how to have winning Christian lives. The good thing about our game is that there are no losers.

On a football team, each member needs to work with the others. He or she needs to pass the ball at the right time and block the other players so the one carrying the ball can get through. Each player has a job to do, and the rest of the team depends on that job getting done. It would be pretty silly if, right before an important game, a member of a football team said, "I don't feel like coming. Go on without me."

Each one of you is just as important. We all have our jobs to do. We all need to be here for our group members. We all need to laugh and learn, to listen and love, to sing and be helpful. A Christian group works together as a team. Will you all be good team members?

2

World Day of Prayer

Object: a toy walkie-talkie
Lesson: Prayer is talking to God.

Outline

Introduce object: Do you know why people call this a walkie-talkie?

1. The name tells you that you can walk (or stand still) and talk to the person on the other unit. We can talk to God any time and any place.
2. God is always ready to hear us.
3. God has special ears so that he can hear all of the people all over the world who love him and talk to him.

Conclusion: God's ears must be very busy and happy today.

Do you know why people call this a walkie-talkie? It is because you can talk on it even when you are walking. You can be walking and talking. That doesn't mean you have to be walking. You can be standing still or sitting as well.

You hold one unit and give your friend the other one. Then you can go where you can't see each other, and you can still talk.

Praying is like having a walkie-talkie with God holding the other unit. Anywhere I go I can talk to God. I can be on my knees by my bed or running down the street or sitting at my desk or working in my yard. Wherever I am, God can hear me.

When you use a walkie-talkie, you have to make sure that the other person can hear you calling him or her. It doesn't do you any good if your friend has gone away and isn't listening for your call. This problem will never happen with God. He is always listening for our call. He is always ready to hear what we have to say. He wants us to talk to him.

Fortunately, God has wonderful ears. He can hear many people talking to him at once. Today is World Day of Prayer. This day is a special day when people everywhere are praying. When we celebrate it, we can think about how people all over the world are talking to God. God's ears must be very busy and happy today.

3

Thanksgiving

Object: toy food
Lesson: We can thank God for so many things.

Outline

Introduce object: I'm glad toy makers make toy food.
1. What if you had only plastic food to eat?
2. What if you didn't have a real house to live in?
3. What if you only had the clothes you are wearing?
4. What if someone in your family were very sick?
5. What if the flowers, birds, and sun were plastic?
Conclusion: God has given us these real things. He just wants us to stop now and then and say, "Thank you, God."

I am glad toy makers make toy food. It doesn't spill and stain the carpet. It doesn't get dried out or moldy or rotten and have to be thrown away. It doesn't attract bugs or small, fast-running animals when it is left out. It is perfect for pretending.

Today we are celebrating Thanksgiving. We are thankful to God every day, but we set aside a certain day to think especially about being thankful.

Let's think again about our food. How would you like to have only toy food to eat? Pretending is fun, but it doesn't fill your stomach when you are really hungry.

What if you didn't have any real food to eat? Chewing on this plastic wouldn't make you feel better. What if you didn't have a real house to live in? You know that there are homeless people. These people have to live in cars or boxes because they don't have a house to live in like you do.

What if you had only the clothes you are wearing right now? They would soon become dirty and worn-out, but you wouldn't have anything else to wear. You would have to keep wearing the dirty, worn-out clothes. Would you like that?

What if someone in your family were very sick? You would need to be helping when you wanted to play. You would need to be quiet all of the time so you wouldn't bother him or her. There would be medicine and doctors.

What if the flowers didn't grow because they were plastic? What if the birds didn't sing because they were plastic? What if the sun were not warm because it was plastic, and there were no raindrops?

But all of these things are real. God has given them to us. He just wants us to stop now and then and say, "Thank you, God."

4

Advent

Object: dominoes

Lesson: Advent is a time of preparing to celebrate the important event of Jesus' birth.

Outline

Introduce object: Do you know what this game is called?
1. Advent, like dominoes, is an ordering or lining up of what is important.
2. It takes special effort for this ordering to happen.
3. Each domino stands for something important in our lives for this season.

Conclusion: What will you do to prepare?

Do you know what this game is called? Yes, it is called dominoes. Usually we play this game by taking turns matching the dots on the little pieces.

There is another way to play with the domino pieces that is just as much fun. You line them all up like this *[demonstrate with a few pieces]*, and then you push the first piece down. As it falls it knocks over the next piece. This goes on until all of the pieces have fallen. If you have enough domino pieces, you can set up a long line all through the house.

Today we are celebrating Advent. Advent is the very beginning of the Christmas season. It is a time of getting ready for the big event. The big event, of course, is Jesus' birth.

Celebrating Advent is like playing the game of dominoes where you line up all of the pieces. It is a time of getting everything in our hearts and minds in order for the important event to come. It is a time of getting ready.

To play dominoes like this you need to concentrate on what you are doing. It takes special effort because, if the pieces are not lined up just right, they will not all fall down.

Some people just let the Christmas season happen to them without thinking much about the real reason for Christmas. They don't think about putting each piece in the right place. They don't think about what Jesus means to them and about how important his birth was.

Let's take some domino pieces now and set them up as we think about what is important in our lives for this season. This piece stands for doing something nice for other people, in Jesus' name, as a present to him. This piece stands for the wonderful Christmas songs we will sing. This piece stands for Advent calendars to help count the days. This one is for manger scenes in our houses. The next pieces are for showing love to those around us, being joyful and bringing happiness, sitting still and thinking about God, hugging someone, saying a special word of kindness to someone, and thinking about the little baby that was born. Now we have a lineup of domino pieces. Did you notice that not one of them stands for all the presents I want for Christmas?

What happens after all the dominoes are lined up in order? Yes, you push down the first one and watch them all fall. What is all our Advent work waiting for? Like the falling of the dominoes, Christmas is the big event. It is the time we celebrate when Jesus was born. What will you do to prepare?

5

Christmas Eve

Object: a newborn baby doll

Lesson: Jesus came to change people's lives.

Outline

Introduce object: Why have you come here on Christmas Eve?
1. What did the shepherds find? A newborn baby.
2. What did the shepherds do? They worshiped him.
3. The shepherds worshiped with the others. They had fellowship.
4. When the shepherds left, they had much to think about.

Conclusion: The baby Jesus came to make a difference in your lives too.

Why have you come here on Christmas Eve? Did you come, like the shepherds, to find a newborn baby? Jesus was born a very long time ago, so we are going to pretend to go back to that time.

What did the shepherds find when they came in search of the baby? They found a tiny baby much like this one, only he was real. He was probably crying a little because that is what newborn babies do.

What did the shepherds do when they found the baby? They worshiped him. We have come to worship him too. We have come to say how wonderful he is. We have come to think about him and tell him how happy we are that he was born. We have come to sings songs to him. Do you

16

feel something warm inside of you? That is the feeling of worship.

The shepherds came to be with the others who loved and worshiped the baby. People still come together every Christmas Eve to fellowship, or love God together. Do you feel like smiling and saying something nice to the people around you? That is the feeling of fellowship.

When the shepherds left, they had much to think about. They had seen the promised baby. It was a wonderful sight. It was a glorious evening. They would remember that night for the rest of their lives. They would never be the same again.

The baby Jesus had changed their lives. The baby Jesus came to make a difference in your lives too.

6

Christmas

Object: a stuffed animal decorated for Christmas

Lesson: We decorate our homes for Christmas. We also need to decorate our hearts.

Outline

Introduce object: This cute, little teddy bear is all dressed up for Christmas.

1. Green is a Christmas color. It stands for living and growing.
2. Red is the other Christmas color. It stands for living blood.
3. True celebration of Christmas comes from the inside.

Conclusion: Do you have Christmas on the inside?

This cute, little teddy bear is all dressed up for Christmas. It has a red dress and little green bows. Do you wear lots of red and green at Christmas time?

The Christmas colors are red and green. Green stands for life. Think of all the green things that are alive and growing. Trees, grass, and plants are all growing. Even in the winter you can find green trees growing outside. They're called evergreens. We have evergreen Christmas trees because they stand for living and growing and remind us that Jesus came to be born as a baby and to live and grow. And just as evergreens are always alive, Jesus lives forever and gives us everlasting life.

The other Christmas color is red. Red stands for blood. Do any of you have blood? Yes, we all have blood inside

18

of us. Without it we could not live and grow. Did the baby Jesus have blood inside of him? Yes, he did. He was a real baby just like us with all the things he needed to grow. What happens when you get a cut? You can see your blood. Drops of red blood come out and run down. Red also stands for the blood that Jesus would lose on the cross.

This little teddy bear is decorated on the outside, but what is on the inside of it? It is stuffed with fluff. It certainly does not have blood or life. It can't really celebrate Christmas because it is not real on the inside. We do a lot of decorating on the outside, but it is the inside that counts. If we don't have Christmas on the inside, we don't really have Christmas. Christmas is loving and singing and being happy and worshiping the baby Jesus—all this is on the inside.

When we see our homes decorated with red and green for Christmas, let's remember to decorate our hearts with the joy of the Christmas season.

Do you have Christmas on the inside?

7

New Year

Object: a new toy

Lesson: We use New Year's to make new promises.

Outline

Introduce object: Here is a brand new toy. The box has never been opened.
1. The toy is new, unopened. This is a new year.
2. We wonder what the toy will look like. We wonder what the new year will bring.
3. What do you plan to do with the toy? What plans can we make for the new year?

Conclusion: At the end of this year, will I find that all of you have kept your promises?

Here is a brand new toy. The box has never been opened. It is like this brand new year. Nobody has ever used it before. It is Megan's toy, and she is sharing it with us. I can't wait to see what is in this box.

I can't wait to begin this new year that God has given us either. Megan thanked the person who gave her this present. We should thank God for giving us a new year to live.

Let's open the box now. I wonder what this new toy will look like. You can't tell very much when it is still in the box. Let's pull it out and look it over. It is a music box with a dancing bear on it. Look how pretty it is.

I wonder what this new year that God has given us will be like. We don't really know what will happen. We don't know what we will do or where we will go or what unexpected things will happen to us.

Megan, how are you going to take care of this music box? Are you going to throw it into your toy box? Will you leave it out in the rain? No, you are going to be careful with it. You don't want to break it. Will you keep it in a special place?

What can we plan to do with this new year? We can promise to do what we are supposed to do and stay out of trouble. We can promise to be extra kind and helpful. We can promise to share and be happy and not pout or throw temper tantrums. We can promise to do the things that we know will make God and our parents happy.

We use New Year's to make new promises. That is a very good way to start the new year. What promises can you make?

Megan, if I come to your house at the end of this year, will I find that you have taken good care of your music box? At the end of this year, will I find that all of you have kept your promises?

8

Epiphany

Object: a puzzle or any toy from which an important piece may be removed

Lesson: The wise men searched a long time for a missing piece to their lives.

Outline

Introduce object: I have just about finished this puzzle, but there seems to be a piece missing.

1. The wise men were troubled by a missing piece in their lives.
2. They were willing to search long and hard for a baby born to be king of the Jews. I will look for the missing piece.
3. They found Jesus and their mission was complete. I found the missing piece and the puzzle is complete.

Conclusion: For us today, Jesus is not that hard to find. We simply need to be willing to open our hearts to him and to love him. Then our lives will be complete.

I have just about finished this puzzle, but there seems to be a piece missing. Let me put in these last few pieces. Yes, there is definitely a hole here. This puzzle won't be any good if I can't find that missing piece. What can I do? Where can I look? I want to find it.

My problem reminds me of the problem that the wise men had many years ago. They were puzzled. They saw an unusual lining up of the planets in the sky and knew that a king was being born to the Jews. They wanted to find that baby, bring him gifts, and worship him. It was like there was a big missing piece in their lives. They wanted so badly to find him that they packed up their camels and prepared for a very long trip. It was hard traveling and took them as long as two years to find this king.

I am willing to look hard for this puzzle piece, but I don't know if I would look for that long. They certainly were determined. When they got close enough to where they thought the baby might be, they began asking if anyone knew where the baby was. Nobody knew, but they still didn't give up. Finally the wise men saw another sign in the sky that showed them where to go. They followed that sign until they came to the house where Jesus was living.

Finding Jesus and worshiping him was like finding a missing piece to their lives. Then their lives were complete—nothing was missing. Wait, I see another puzzle piece in my bag. Let's see if it is the right one. Yes, my puzzle is complete—nothing is missing.

The wise men had finished their trip. They had searched for a long time and traveled far, but they had found Jesus.

For us today, Jesus is not that hard to find. We simply need to be willing to open our hearts to him and to love him. Then our lives will be complete.

9

Lent

Object: a toy broom, mop, or vacuum cleaner
Lesson: Lent is a time of cleaning and preparing our hearts for Easter.

Outline

Introduce object: This floor is dirty. I need this broom to clean it. (Introduce Lent.)
1. We clean bits and pieces of things from the floor. We clean our hearts as well.
2. We feel better when we are clean.
3. We have more room for good thoughts when we are clean. We can think about what Easter means.

Conclusion: What will you do to clean up?

This floor is dirty. I need this broom to clean it. Cleaning reminds me of the special time of year this is. This is the beginning of the season before Easter called Lent. Lent is the time we prepare our hearts and minds for celebrating Easter. Do you remember what we call the time when we start getting ready for Christmas? Yes, that is called Advent.

Just as there are bits of things on this floor that need sweeping away, so there are bits of things in our hearts that need cleaning out. Let's get rid of some bad thoughts *[sweep as you talk]*. Here is an "I want what my friend has" thought that needs to be cleaned. Oh, this is an "I'm mad at my brother" thought. Let's get rid of that. And the ever

24

popular "I'm going to tease my little sister" thought. That certainly has to go. Over here is a selfish "give me, give me" that doesn't belong in a clean heart. An "I don't want to do my chores" thought is here too along with some "let's get even" thoughts. All these thoughts have to go.

Why do we clean this floor? We like a clean floor. It makes us feel good. It looks nice. Why do we clean our hearts to get ready for Easter? It is even more important to be clean on the inside. You feel better. You look better. You have more room for good thoughts. Let's think of some good thoughts [take suggestions].

We also have room to think about what Easter means. We have room and time to remember that Jesus loved us so much that he was willing to die for us. We need lots of room for all that love.

What does Lent mean? Yes, Lent is the time to clean up all the little corners of our heart to get ready for Easter. What will you do to clean up?

10

Palm Sunday

Object: a toy microphone (some come with dolls)

Lesson: On Palm Sunday we celebrate Jesus' triumphant entry into Jerusalem.

Outline

Introduce object: (Introduce Palm Sunday.) To be loud today we can use microphones.

1. We can have fun remembering Jesus' triumphant entry. It was an exciting time.
2. We remember that Jesus came to do something very important; but it wasn't to be king, it was to die for us.
3. This message is given through many microphones in churches today.

Conclusion: We can shout about the real reason Jesus came.

Today we are talking about Palm Sunday. Do you know what that is? It is the day when Jesus rode into Jerusalem. He rode on a donkey (they didn't have convertibles at that time). The people all thought that he had come to save them from Roman rulers and to be their king, so they all yelled and waved palm branches. They were so excited. Each one tried to yell louder than the next. I wonder what they did to make themselves sound the loudest.

To be loud today we can use microphones. I have one here. Let's see how loud I can be. Now let's see how loud you can be with just your voices. Everybody shout, "Yeah! Here comes Jesus!" Now imagine you are waving something in your hands to get Jesus' attention. Jump up and down. You are all excited. This is fun. Usually people don't like us to be noisy.

It was fun and exciting to be there when Jesus came into Jerusalem. It is still fun and exciting today to remember. We remember that Jesus came to do something very important. Did he come to be king of the Jews? No, the important thing he came to do was to die for us. Now that is a message that should be shouted through the microphone. In fact, it is. That same message is being shouted through microphones in churches all over the world today.

We remember Palm Sunday because it was a time when everybody knew that Jesus was important and special. Just as those people shouted about Jesus then, we do now. We can shout about the real reason Jesus came.

Easter

Object: a plastic toy egg that opens

Lesson: An egg reminds us of many things on Easter.

Outline

Introduce object: How many of you have plastic eggs like this one in your house?

1. Why do we talk about an egg? An egg is a symbol of new life.
2. Why do we have an empty egg? The tomb was empty.
3. Will we leave this egg empty? We can fill it with good things and ourselves with good thoughts.

Conclusion: Most of all, we can think of Jesus' great love. This great love is why we have Easter.

How many of you have plastic eggs like this one in your house? They come in all colors and different sizes. Many people use them for Easter egg hunts.

Why do we talk about eggs at Easter? We color eggs. We hide eggs and roll eggs. We get candy eggs. Why are eggs special? The egg is a sign of new life. When an egg hatches, what do you get? That's right, you get a chick or a baby bird or some other small animal. Why do we talk about new life at Easter? Because Jesus rose from the grave and has new life; because Jesus died for our sins and gives us new life.

Why do I have an empty egg? It can help remind us of something else we talk about today. Do you remember how the women went to Jesus' tomb early in the morning so that they could take care of his dead body? What did they find when they got there? The tomb was empty, just like this empty egg. Jesus had risen. Jesus was gone. He was alive again.

This egg is empty, but it is meant to be filled. What can we put inside of it? Candy or a small toy would fit. If we had an empty spot inside of us, what would be good to fill it with right now? We would want kind and happy thoughts. One good thought to keep in your hearts and remember is that Jesus loves you very, very much.

When you see an egg, you can be reminded of many things on Easter. Most of all, think of Jesus' great love for you. This great love is why we have Easter.

12

Pentecost

Object: balloons

Lesson: The Holy Spirit came to the believers on Pentecost and is with believers today.

Outline

Introduce object: Who would like to help me by blowing up a balloon? (Introduce Pentecost.)

1. I have a balloon for everyone. The Holy Spirit came to all believers.
2. You can fill your balloon a little or a lot. You can choose to be filled a little or a lot.
3. You can do more with the full balloons. The Holy Spirit gives power to do more.

Conclusion: Let the Holy Spirit fill you, as he filled those believers long ago.

Who would like to help me by blowing up a balloon? I brought these balloons to help me tell you about Pentecost. When Jesus went back into heaven, he promised the people who believed in him that he would send a comforter, someone who could always be with them and help them. Jesus, who is smarter than we can ever imagine, knew that it would be best if this comforter were not a body, like you and I have, but a power.

The believers were waiting for this comforter. When he came, they were nearly knocked over from his power. First there came a sound like a strong rushing wind. Then flames

30

of fire like those from a candle sat on their heads but didn't burn them. Just think how surprised they were. Then the believers started speaking in the languages of other countries. Imagine being able to speak another language without ever studying it! You can see why we need a special day to remember and celebrate this event.

I have a balloon here for each of you. The Holy Spirit came to all the believers. His power was for each of them.

You can choose to fill your balloon with as little or as much air as you want. The Holy Spirit is still here, and believers can fill themselves with a little or a lot of his exciting power. How do you fill yourself? You pray and ask for this power. Then you use the power to live happier, more helpful Christian lives. You feel this power within you, and you listen to the small voice that tells you what to do and how to bring happiness.

Now that the balloons are filled, you can do more with them. You can play with them, decorate with them, or give them to someone to cheer up him or her. Christians can do more with the power of the Holy Spirit within them. They can live more exciting lives. Pentecost is a wonderful day to celebrate. Let the Holy Spirit fill you, as he filled those believers long ago.

13

Mother's Day

Object: a soft, cuddly, stuffed toy

Lesson: Mother's Day is a time to remember and appreciate a mother's love. (Note: If any of the children are not being raised by their mother, alter the lesson to include grandmother, etc.)

Outline

Introduce object: I love these soft, cuddly toys.
1. Mothers are soft and cuddly.
2. Mothers are also stern when necessary.
3. Remember how much your mother loves you.

Conclusion: How many of you will give your mother a very special hug today?

I love these soft, squeezable, cuddly toys. They just make you want to hug them.

Mothers are known for being soft and cuddly. They hug you when you hurt yourself. They cuddle you when you are upset. They stop and listen when you have a story to tell. They put their arms around you and read you stories. They listen to your prayers. They kiss you good night and tuck you into your bed. They hug you tightly and say how much they will miss you when you leave or when they have to leave.

This extra-soft toy cannot do much besides be hugged. Not that hugging isn't important, but mothers can do much more. Who do we run to when we need a bandage?

Our mother. Who do we want when we are sick? Our mother. Who makes us food when we are hungry? Our mother. Who drives us to our friend's house? Our mother. Who settles our fights? Our mother. Who makes us go to bed early if we have done something wrong? Our mother. Who punishes us for using bad words? Our mother. Who yells at us for running into the street? Our mother. Sometimes a mother's job is tough, and she has to be tough.

Whatever she does, she does it because she loves you. She wants to do her job of being a mother as well as possible. Today is a special day to remember what she does and to thank her for doing her job even when it is difficult. Today is a day to thank her for her very great love.

How many of you will give your mother a very special hug today?

Father's Day

Object: a toy catcher's glove (or bat and baseball)

Lesson: Father's Day is a time to remember and appreciate our fathers.

Outline

Introduce object: Is your father the one who plays catch with you?

1. Your father teaches you the rules of the game.
2. Your father teaches you to keep your eye on the ball.
3. Your father teaches you to do your best.

Conclusion: Be sure to thank your father today.

Fathers and mothers do many of the same things these days to help care for their children. Is your father the one who plays catch with you? If not, you will just have to pretend for a minute that he does. You can tell me later about something special your father teaches you. If you don't have a father, you can think about a grandfather or an uncle.

When you practice baseball, your father teaches you the rules of the game. Fathers also teach you about the rules of your life. A good father teaches you to love God and to respect other people. He teaches you to do the right thing even when it is hard for you.

When you practice baseball, your father teaches you to keep your eye on the ball. In order to bat or to catch the ball, you need to know where it is. A good father also teaches you to keep your eye on God. If you are looking at him, you will live your life the way you should.

Your father teaches you to do your best. Winning is important, but it isn't everything. Playing the game well is what counts. A good father teaches you to live your life as a Christian the best you can. He teaches you to use God's help to do this. God gave you your father to advise you. It is up to you to follow what he says.

Fathers have a big job. Even if your father doesn't live with you, he still has a big responsibility. I'm glad we have a special day to appreciate all our fathers do and to thank them. Be sure to thank your father today.

15

World Communion Sunday

Object: round balls of different colors and sizes
Lesson: People all over the world love and worship God.

Outline

Introduce object: (Introduce World Communion Sunday.) I have several different kinds of balls here.
1. People all over the world play with balls (celebrate communion).
2. Balls come in different sizes. So do people.
3. Balls come in different colors. So do people.
4. Balls are round. Communion helps us round our edges.

Conclusion: I'm so happy that people all over the world celebrate communion. Remember them today.

Today we are talking about World Communion Sunday, a day when people all over the world celebrate communion and think about how Jesus died on the cross for them. I have several different kinds of balls here: a tennis ball, a baseball, a soccer ball, and a beach ball. People all over the world play ball. Many of their ball games are like the ones we play. Some are a little different. People all over the world celebrate communion. Many of the things they do are like what we do. Some are different.

Balls come in different sizes. People come in different sizes also. You are short people. God loves short people.

To celebrate communion you can be any size or anybody. You just need to love Jesus.

Balls come in different colors. You might have a favorite color, but does the color of this beach ball make it bounce better? This one has a pretty good bounce. Do you suppose that is because it is yellow? No, the color doesn't make a bit of difference. People come in different colors too. When you look all the way around the world, you find every color of people that God made. It is wonderful to think of people of different colors loving Jesus.

All of these balls are round. Being round is what a ball is all about. It has no edges or sharp corners. You can throw it because it is round. You can bounce it because it is round. Celebrating communion is like being round in our hearts. We get rid of our edges and corners—our unkind thoughts or harmful actions. Communion is the rounding of our souls and the promise to live more like Jesus.

I'm so happy that people all over the world celebrate communion. Remember them today.

16

Missions Sunday

Object: the game in which children sit in a row and pass along a message

Lesson: On Missions Sunday we think about telling the world about God's love.

Outline

Introduce object: Today we are going to play a game. (Introduce Missions Sunday.)

1. It doesn't work to pass the message along. Someone needs to go.
2. Those who have gone need our prayers.
3. I have to go myself if I want to give someone the message.

Conclusion: Would you be willing to be God's messenger?

Today we are going to play a game. Everyone sit next to each other in a long row. I am going to say something to Danny, and Danny will say it to Crissy, and so on. We will do this until the message has passed all the way down the row to the last person. Then we will ask the last person what he or she heard. Now, I have to say this very quietly because the game only works if the person you are talking to is the only one who hears what is being said. [*Whisper something like,* "I'm glad you are here today."] Sometimes we get the message right, and sometimes it gets distorted. Let's try another message. [*Say,* "Jesus loves you. Tell the world."]

Today is Missions Sunday. It is a day to pray for the people who have gone to other lands to help other people and to tell them that Jesus loves them. It is also a day to think about telling others ourselves about Jesus.

In our game, we had a little trouble telling a simple message in just one row. Just think if this message had to be brought all the way to another country by people passing the word along like we did. Even if we could shout the message to the next person in line, it wouldn't work to go far away like that. Someone needs to go tell the message.

Our message didn't get through quite right. The message we bring to others needs to be clear and true and loving and helpful. It is not easy to make the message that way. The people who have gone to give God's message need our prayers that they can do this.

It would have been better for me to have given the message to the last person in line myself. If I want to give God's message to other people, I have to go to them myself. God want us to tell the world of his love. Would you be willing to be God's messenger?

17
Faith

Object: an electronic game
Lesson: Faith is believing completely in God.

Outline

Introduce object: Danny loaned me this electronic game.
1. I believe that this game works. I believe that God is real.
2. I will be able to do more with this game when I learn more about it. Faith grows with knowledge.
3. I do not understand how this game works. Faith is believing in something even when you do not know how it works.

Conclusion: Believe in God and love him with your whole heart.

Danny loaned me this electronic game. It plays baseball. He is teaching me how to work it.

Today we are talking about faith. Do you know what faith is? It is believing completely in God. I know that this game is real. I have seen people work this game and have even tried this game myself. I found that it works just the way the box says it does and just the way Danny says it does. I know God is real too. I can see God in the beautiful world he gave us. I can read about him in the Bible. I can learn about him from my friends. I have tried believing in God completely, and I know that he is just like he says he is.

There are more things this electronic game can do that I still need to learn. It will take me quite a while to learn them all. I don't know all there is to know about God either. Every day I learn something new and wonderful about God. I think and read and pray. My faith in him grows deeper. It's exciting that I still don't know all there is to know about God. It keeps me looking for answers and wanting to learn more.

I must admit that I don't understand how this electronic game works. There is some kind of computer chip in here that stores the information. I really don't understand computer chips, but I don't have to know how the game works to use it. I can learn to play it as well as a computer expert can. Faith means that you believe in God even though you don't understand how he works. It is enough to know that God works. If God tells me to do something, I know it is best for me to do it. If God sends something into my life, I know it is for a reason.

Even though we don't know everything about God or understand him completely, we can believe in him completely. Have faith. Believe in God and love him with your whole heart.

18

Hope

Object: a toy fire engine

Lesson: Jesus is our hope.

Outline

Introduce object: How many of you have a fire engine?
1. Hope means having a reason to think things will get better.
2. Jesus is our hope for the world.

Conclusion: We have every reason to feel good about life because we have hope.

How many of you have a fire engine? It is exciting to think of rushing to a fire and putting it out, saving the house and helping the people.

Today I want to talk about hope. Hope means that we have a reason to think that things will be better. A fire is a terrible thing. Knowing that there is a fire engine on the way means that there is hope that the fire can be put out, perhaps before there is too much damage. We know enough about fire engines to know that they will come quickly with sirens sounding. The firemen will work hard and use all of their equipment to put out the fire. If anybody can do it, they can. If anybody will do it, they will.

Jesus gives us hope. When we feel our worst, we have hope that things will get better because Jesus loves us. We can hope or expect that Jesus will help us. We know that he is all-powerful and that he wants what is best for us. We know he can and will do what is best for us.

Jesus is our hope for the world. He is our fire engines and police cars and judges and presidents, our smartest and hardest-working people, all rolled into one. We have every reason to feel good about life because we have hope.

19

Love

Object: the blood pressure cuff from a child's medical kit
Lesson: God's love flows through us into every part of our lives.

Outline

Introduce object: (Describe how to take someone's blood pressure.)
1. The love of God is like the oxygen in your blood; it is necessary for life.
2. This love, like the oxygen in our blood, must flow through us and reach all the little parts of our lives.
Conclusion: Is God's love flowing all through you?

How many of you have had the doctor take your blood pressure? Did he or she use something that looks like this? The doctor puts this cuff around your arm snugly and then pinches this little pump, which tightens the cuff until it gives your arm a big hug. Finally, the doctor looks at this gauge to see what your blood pressure is. The gauge tells the doctor how the blood is pushing against the walls of the blood vessels as it moves through your body.

Why does the doctor check your blood pressure? He needs to make sure the blood is moving the way it should. If your blood pressure is too high or too low, it means that something is wrong. The blood needs to travel evenly to reach your whole body because it carries the oxygen that you need to live. Can you live without breathing? No, the oxygen that you breathe into your body is necessary for your life. And this oxygen travels in your blood to all the parts of your body. If the oxygen does not reach a part of your body, that part will die.

God's love is like the oxygen that is carried in our blood. It is necessary for Christian life. It flows through us and makes us alive Christians.

Just as the blood needs to carry oxygen to every part of our body, so too the love of God needs to reach every part of us so that we can have complete and healthy Christian lives. We can't keep any secret sins or wrong things tucked away in the corners of our Christian lives. The love of God needs to reach every little cell, every little word, thought, and feeling to give us what we need to survive.

When your blood is flowing the way it should, you feel great. It is also a good feeling to have a healthy, well-nourished Christian life by having God's love all through you. Is God's love flowing all through you?

Faith, Hope, and Love

Object: two flashlights, one with batteries removed
Lesson: Strength comes from the inside.

Outline

Introduce object: We have all used a flashlight at one time or another.
   1. The best one is the one that works.
   2. Flashlights work by batteries. Our batteries are faith, hope, and love.
   3. We need to keep our batteries recharged or replaced.
Conclusion: Are your batteries charged?

We have all used a flashlight at one time or another. How many of you have your own flashlight? I use mine to see outside in the dark. I use it to see inside when the electricity goes off. I use it to read the water meter in the dark corner of the basement. I use it to help me look for something in the attic. I may use it just for fun, but I would never shine it in somebody's eyes.

I have two flashlights here. Which one do you think is the best? The biggest one might be the best. Let's turn it on. It doesn't seem to work. Do you still think it is the best? The best one is the one that works. The smaller one is working. The same is true of people: The better one is the one who works—the one who shines out to others by doing good.

Why does this flashlight work? If we look inside the flashlights, we will see that there are batteries in the one that works. There are no batteries in the other one. Do you suppose that there is also something special inside the people who work? Yes, they have batteries filled with God's love. Let's call these batteries faith, hope, and love. The Bible tells us that it is very important to have faith, hope, and love inside us. Faith, hope, and love give us the power to shine out with warmth and kindness and goodness to others.

Batteries are portable power. They store electricity so that you can use it when you need it. When the batteries are used up, you need to get new ones. There are also rechargeable batteries. They can be hooked up to the electricity in your home and restored. From time to time our inner batteries—our faith, hope, and love—need to be replaced or recharged. We replace or recharge them by plugging into God's power through going to church, reading the Bible, praying, studying, and fellowshiping. These activities keep our lights shining brightly. Are your batteries charged?

21

Joy

Object: children's bath bubbles or any liquid soap (put about a teaspoon of soap in a glass half filled with water) and a straw or bubble pipe

Lesson: Joy comes from within and overflows and spills onto others.

Outline

Introduce object: I love to make bubbles.
1. Joy, like bubbles, comes from the inside.
2. Joy fills our lives like the bubbles fill the glass.
3. Joy overflows onto others like the bubbles overflow the glass.

Conclusion: Are you a joyful Christian?

I love to make bubbles. Watch what happens when I blow through this straw into this glass of water. The bubbles rise quickly to the top and keep right on going.

Christians are joyful people. They have a great deal to be happy about. They spend much time rejoicing. Right in the middle of that word *rejoicing* you can hear the little word *joy*. These bubbles remind me of joy.

Joy comes from inside us like these bubbles come from inside this glass. Each little bubble is a happiness that God gives. There are bubbles for songs I enjoyed; some for sharing laughter with a friend; bigger ones for good things I have heard. There are bubbles for things I have learned.

It's not long before my glass is full of bubbles, just as my life is full of the good things God gives. The flowers, trees, sunshine, and scampering squirrels bring me joy. Hugs, happy words, and kind actions make my cup so full that it can't hold all the joy.

Now the bubbles are spilling out and down the glass. This joy that I have is bubbling out of me and flowing onto others. Joy is contagious. Others are becoming joyful. Do you like to be around happy people? Is it fun to be with someone who is bubbly? Do you like sharing in the joy of another person? Joys are better when they are shared. A beautiful day is a nice thing. When you share the beautiful day, it becomes bubblingly wonderful.

Christians are to have joy that overflows and spills onto others. Are you a joyful Christian?

22

Patience

Object: a toy caterpillar or one made with an egg carton
Lesson: God's plans may require our patience.

Outline

Introduce object: Did you ever watch a caterpillar walk?
  1. The caterpillar going at its own pace teaches us patience.
  2. We must be willing to wait for many things in life.
  3. God will give the caterpillar wings.
Conclusion: We must wait for God's time.

Did you ever watch a caterpillar walk? The other day Megan, Sean, and I watched a caterpillar make its way down the driveway. We thought it would be interesting to find out where the little caterpillar wanted to go. We watched for several minutes while the caterpillar busied its way over sticks and around stones on the driveway. After about fifteen minutes, the caterpillar had only gone a few feet from where we had first seen it.

The caterpillar gives us a good lesson in patience. The children and I wanted the caterpillar to get to where it was going while we were watching it. We wanted it to go in our time. We grew tired of watching it go its own pace. We get tired of waiting in our own lives as well. We want God to give us everything now or even sooner, but God makes us wait for the answers to some of our prayers.

50

There is an expression, "Good things come to those who wait," that means there are many things we have to wait for. You won't enjoy a cake before it is baked. If you don't take your time and put a kite together correctly, it will crash and break when you try to fly it. You must take the time to earn money before you can spend it. You won't be big enough or know enough to drive a car until you are older. When you ask a question, you need to give the person you asked enough time to answer it.

The caterpillar was making very slow progress when we were watching it. But God has something wonderful planned for the caterpillar. Soon it will spin a cocoon, and when it is ready, it will be a moth or a butterfly. God has wonderful plans for us. But we must wait until they are ready. We must be patient. We must wait for God's time.

Self-Control

Object: a battery operated toy
Lesson: God wants his children to control themselves.

Outline

Introduce object: This little dog is supposed to jump up and down and bark.

1. Life has problems. It is not fair.
2. Self-control means not overreacting.
3. Self-control means being calm enough to solve problems.

Conclusion: The next time you feel like getting really angry, stop and think, then control yourself.

This little dog is supposed to jump up and down and bark. Okay, dog, do your thing. I'll give it a little tap. Perhaps it will work if I pick it up and shake it. It is still not working. This is making me mad. What if I throw it against the wall? I'm getting so angry I could drop it on the floor and stomp on it.

Let's take a look at what is happening here. First of all, the toy isn't working. That's a real problem. Life is full of problems. These problems are not spread out evenly either. Life is not fair. Good people try to be fair, but life itself is not. We wouldn't need so much of God's help if life were always fair.

Second, my reaction to the toy not working was to get angry. Did I need to get so upset? Did it do me any good to get so upset? What if I had broken the toy because I was so angry? My reaction to the broken toy did not show self-control. I got angry and could have done something foolish. Do you think God wants us to become angry about every little thing? Of course not. Self-control means not overreacting to life's problems. That includes not getting angry quickly, not saying something we shouldn't because we let ourselves get too upset, and not hurting someone or something because of our anger. When you have self-control, nobody has to tell you to calm down because you already have the sense to do the right thing.

When you have self-control, you can think about your problem and how to solve it. Let me take a closer look at this toy dog. I see the problem: The battery is missing. How could I possibly expect this to work when there is no battery? If I had not had self-control, I could have broken a perfectly good toy.

God wants us all to have self-control and to use the good brains he gave us to solve problems. The next time you feel like getting really angry, stop and think, then control yourself.

Trust

Object: a swing (most swings are detachable) or a long, thick rope with knots tied near one end

Lesson: Trust means having confidence in God.

Outline

Introduce object: We have this rope swing tied to a tall tree in our backyard.
1. Trust the swing to hold you. Trust God.
2. Trust the swing to travel in a set pattern. Trust God to keep his promises.
3. We like the swing to go higher and higher. We will live more exciting Christian lives if we want God to do more with us.
4. Hold on tightly to the swing and to God.

Conclusion: Trust in God. Know that he is true and faithful.

We have this rope swing tied to a tall tree in our backyard. Our grandchildren swing way out across the yard on this long rope. They exhaust their grandparents with pleas to be pushed more and more.

Today I want to talk about trust. When you go on a swing, you trust the swing to hold you. You get on and know that the rope or chain is strong enough to hold you. We trust in God. We know that he is strong enough to hold us.

When you get on a swing, you trust that the swing will take you back and forth. You know where it will go because you have seen it. You are not going to fly over the house on the swing. You are not going to crash into the garage. The swing will go back and forth in about the same place. When we put our trust in God, we know what to expect. We know God will take care of us. We know he will do what is best for us. We trust him to guide us. We trust him to keep us where we should be. We know he will keep his promises.

When someone is on a swing, he or she often says, "Push me higher." We like to go higher and higher. The higher we go, the more exciting it is. The more we trust God, the more we want to swing out and do things for him, the more we want our lives to count for something. The more we trust God to use us, the more exciting our lives are.

Now, when you are swinging, you need to hold on tightly. If you don't, you might fall off and get hurt. Would that be the swing's fault? No, it would be your fault for not doing what you know you should be doing. So too, when you are trusting God, you hold on tightly to his promises and his will for your life. Don't let go; don't slip and fall and miss the fun. That will hurt your life.

Trust means having confidence in God and his promises. Trust in God. Know that he is true and faithful.

25

Christian Vision

Object: the eye chart from a child's medical kit
Lesson: See and know clearly and have a vision for the future.

Outline

Introduce object: (Describe the use of the eye chart.)
1. You can see and know what is around you.
2. You can see when something is wrong.
3. You can have a vision for the future.
Conclusion: That's good Christian eyesight.

How well can you see? When you go to the doctor's office for a checkup, he or she will look at your eyes and usually have you read a chart on the wall. Most charts look like this one. You start with the big letters across the top and see if you can read them all. If you don't know your letters, the doctor has a chart with all *E*s on it. You tell him which way they are pointing. If you can't read enough of the chart, he sends you to an eye doctor with better equipment to check your eyes.

You are careful with your eyes because you want to be able to see well for a very long time. When you can see around you, you know what is going on. When you can see well as a Christian, you know what is right. When you can see well as a Christian, you know what to do.

If you can really see as a Christian, you know when something is wrong. If someone asks you to help her cheat, you will know not to do it. If you are tempted to lie, you will see that it is the wrong thing to do. If you are about to say something unkind to a person, you can see that it will hurt his feelings. If you are tempted to take something that is not yours, you can see that it is stealing.

We say that a person with good eyes has good vision. We also talk about vision as what we know or hope for the future. Do you have something you want to do with your life? Do you have a vision for your family, perhaps loving God and being loving to each other? Then you have a vision that you can pray, think, and work toward. I have a vision that we are all happy, loving and singing and praising God.

See and know what is right and have a vision or hope for the future. That's good Christian eyesight.

26

Choosing Friends

Object: watercolors, water, and paper

Lesson: You will become like your companions.

Outline

Introduce object: I like to paint with watercolors.

1. When you overlap blue and yellow, you get green. Good friends bring out the best in each other.
2. When you overlap purple and yellow, you get more purple. Bad friends begin to teach you bad things.
3. One sloppy color can ruin the painting. One unkind or uncooperative person can ruin the group.

Conclusion: This time I will be more careful. Are you going to be careful when choosing friends?

I like to paint with watercolors. You need to get your brush very wet to get a color ready. When you change colors you rinse your brush. Does anyone know what happens if you don't rinse your brush?

I brought watercolors to help me talk about choosing companions, or friends. Just as in painting with watercolors, you need to be careful about what you are doing. You need to choose friends whom you want to be like, because when you spend a lot of time with someone, you become more like that person.

Now I have two colors that I am working with in my picture, blue and yellow. Let's say these two colors are playing together. I'll put a line of blue down my paper and a line of yellow right next to it *[overlap]*. Look what happens to my colors. The place where the two colors touch has become green. This is an example of two good, clean colors playing together. Like two good friends, they play happily and learn good things from each other. They become a little like each other because they share, talk, play games, help each other with chores, and do things for other people.

Now my yellow color has gone to play with a purple color. I'll paint a big stripe of yellow and a purple one next to it *[overlap]*. You can see a lot of purple and some brown, but yellow has pretty well gotten lost. The purple has taken over. Now let me tell you something about the purple color. Sometimes this person can be okay, but often there is selfishness and meanness in his heart. This person tells lies and sometimes steals. If yellow hangs around with him, yellow may begin to do these things too. Together they might start with ringing a doorbell and running away, or making crank phone calls. Then purple might convince yellow that it is all right to take a little something that doesn't belong to them. Soon they will be telling lies to their parents about where they are going. Purple is taking over. Purple is not a good companion. Yellow should not hang around with purple. Yellow needs to choose a better friend.

Sometimes one person can ruin a whole group *[paint a big wet frown face and hold up the picture so that the paint runs down the page]*. Then the group needs to say, "Play right or leave."

I'm going to have to start over again with my picture. This time I will be more careful. Are you going to be careful when choosing friends?

27

Commitment

Object: a toy airplane

Lesson: God wants us to make commitments and keep them.

Outline

Introduce object: Have you ever flown in a real airplane?
1. Decide to be a passenger. Decide to be a Christian.
2. Decide which airplane to take and where to go. Make a commitment to a church or group or program.
3. You can't get off the plane until it lands. You must not leave the commitment.

Conclusion: God wants us to make commitments and keep them.

Have you ever flown in a real airplane? It is fun to fly up into the air and see all the houses and cars and roads becoming smaller and smaller. Then you fly up into and over the clouds *[demonstrate with toy plane].*

Flying in a plane reminds me of making a commitment. A commitment is a promise or pledge to do something. When you decide to ride in an airplane, you make a commitment to be a passenger. When a person becomes a Christian, he or she makes a commitment by saying, "I want to love God with all my heart and to do whatever Jesus wants me to do." Did you know that there are some people who are afraid to ride in airplanes? They are afraid of making the commitment to be a passenger on an airplane. They are missing out on a lot of fun. Some people are afraid to make a commitment to Jesus too. They're also missing out on a lot of fun.

Once you have decided that you want to ride in an airplane, you need to decide which plane to take. There may be many airplanes that are going where you want to go. Which one is best? Christians have decisions to make also. They join groups and programs and churches. Joining a group is a commitment, as you know by being here with your group. Christians may be asked by their group to work on a project. You may be asked to help with a lesson or a program or a party. God wants you to make commitments or promises to help.

Now if you were up in an airplane, would you say, "Wait a minute. I quit. I don't want to do this anymore"? It's silly to think that someone is going to try to get off an airplane in the middle of a flight. It is a good idea to think of your promise, or commitment, in the same way. Once you have made it, there is no quitting. You stay on the plane until it gets to where it is going. You stay with your promise until the job is done.

God wants us to make commitments and keep them.

28

Controlling Your Emotions

Object: the toy thermometer from a child's medical kit
Lesson: We have an emotional as well as a physical temperature.

Outline

Introduce object: Can you tell me what this is?
1. A slight temperature is like being irritated.
2. A high fever is dangerous, as is extreme emotion.
3. A low temperature is like being cold emotionally.

Conclusion: Feelings are something that we want to keep even, like our body temperature, so that we can live a happy Christian life.

Can you tell me what this is? It takes your temperature. It is called a thermometer. When would your mother or a doctor use a real thermometer with you? When they think you are sick.

If your temperature is too high, you have a fever. How can this thermometer tell if you have a fever? There are numbers on the side that say what your temperature is. Does anyone know what your body temperature should be? About 98.6 is normal. For some people it is a little less. If you have a fever, you might run a slight temperature of 99 or 100. If it gets to 101, 102, or 103, it gets more serious, and something needs to be done about it. If it gets over 104, it is very serious. You are very sick.

You have an emotional temperature also. Emotions are your feelings. If you are feeling calm and happy, you do not have an emotional fever. You might get a slight case of irritation or get mad about something for a minute or two and then get over it. You might cry about something and then it is all right again. That happens.

If, however, you get very angry, and your emotional temperature continues to build, that's not good. You don't want to let your emotional temperature climb and climb. You need to do something to get it lowered. You need to talk about what's making you angry. You need to solve the problem. You need to get your feelings under control. If you let your emotions get hotter and hotter, you might explode and do or say something you will regret. Just like a fever of 104 or more, an emotional fever is dangerous.

Sometimes temperatures fall lower than they should be. If you are out in the cold for a long time, your body temperature might begin to go down. This is also a problem. It is called hypothermia. Your body can't act normally if its temperature gets too low. You need to get warmed up. If you have no feelings or very cold feelings, there is also a problem. You won't be able to show love and joy. You will not be concerned about other people. These feelings need to be warmed up by the love of God.

Being too hot or cold in our emotions makes our life unhappy. Feelings are something that we want to keep even, like our body temperature, so that we can live a happy Christian life.

29

Cooperation

Object: roller blades or roller skates

Lesson: For a program to run smoothly, all participants must cooperate.

Outline

Introduce object: How many of you have roller blades?

1. If one wheel does not cooperate, the skate stops. One member not cooperating can ruin the group.
2. One wheel going too slowly will slow the skate. One member not cooperating will interfere with the group.
3. There is no free ride if you are a wheel. Jesus wants us to do our share.

Conclusion: Do you cooperate?

How many of you have roller blades? When I was young, we all used roller skates. Beginners still tend to use skates with wheels in that position. It is easier to stand on them. It must also be easier on the ankles.

I want you to take a careful look at these wheels because I would like to talk about cooperation. Have you ever had a wheel that decided not to cooperate? I did once. When I was a teenager, I was skating along quite fast with a group of other teenagers in a roller rink. All of a sudden I was no longer skating. One wheel had broken down, and the whole skate would not work. I lost my balance completely, so the other skate couldn't work. The skates went up, and I crashed to the floor and skidded into a wall.

Since I had fallen in front of a large group of people my age, it made a lasting impression on me. Someone helped me up and I limped over to a bench. Upon examination I discovered one broken wheel. I could hardly believe that one wheel had caused all that trouble.

Cooperation means that all the members of a group join in what the group is doing. Just one person not doing his or her job can stop the whole group. Imagine a whole group project coming to a crashing halt because one person decided not to go along with it. What if one person in your group kept arguing—wouldn't that spoil the whole group? What if one person wouldn't do his or her work? Then everybody's job would have to change to include some of that person's work.

In the case of these skates, one wheel going too slowly will cause a problem for the whole group of wheels as well. What if two people were turning a jump rope and one decided to go slower? The jumper couldn't jump. What if two people were rowing a boat and one went more slowly? The boat would begin to go in circles.

There is no free ride if you are a roller skate wheel. You have to do your part and turn. Jesus wants us to get along, to do our share, to finish our job, to help the group. Do you cooperate?

30

Counting Your Blessings

Object: a bag of marbles

Lesson: There are good reasons for thinking about the good things God has given you.

Outline

Introduce object: Sean brought a bag of marbles for us to see today.

1. Count your blessings to remember and know all that God has given you.
2. Count your blessings so that you will be focused on the positive things of your life.
3. Count your blessings so that you will be too busy for less productive tasks.

Conclusion: Do you count your blessings?

Sean brought a bag of marbles for us to see today. Thank you for sharing them. When I was young, we used to sort and count our marbles regularly. The larger ones were more valuable, as were the clear ones that we called "puries." We played games in which, if you were able to shoot your marble and bump it into the other person's marble, then you got to keep the other's marble. Then we counted the marbles all over again.

Counting your blessings, like counting your marbles, is also a fun thing to do. Blessings are good things in your life. It is fun to count them because then we can know and remember all the good things that God has given us.

I can think of and thank God for my wonderful family and my job of teaching, which I enjoy. I can count my health and ability to travel. I can appreciate all the good people in my life who are so kind to me. I can count the beautiful things in nature: trees, butterflies, fireflies, birds, squirrels, rabbits, deer, and many more. I can count sunny days and exciting thunderstorms. There are so many things to count. What did I miss?

Another reason for counting your blessings is that it keeps you thinking about all the good things in the world. There are always bad things happening, and if we can help any of the bad things, we should think about them. But we should only think about how to make them better. Then the bad things become blessings to count. Just thinking about one bad thing after another is not good for us. It is not what God wants us to do.

Counting your blessings keeps you happy and content. Counting your blessings gives you something to do. It helps you fall asleep at night. It keeps your mind busy. It is a good way to pass the time. It is a good way for us to search our hearts and minds. It is good use of our energy.

There are good reasons for thinking about the good things God has given you. Do you count your blessings?

31

Encouragement

Object: a toy syringe from a child's medical kit
Lesson: We need encouragement for successful Christian living.

Outline

Introduce object: (Describe the syringe.)
1. We get shots for immunization. Christians immunize with peace, joy, hope, and love.
2. We get shots of medicine. Some situations call for shots of encouragement, sharing, love, patience, honesty, and faith.
3. We get shots from the doctor. We get shots for Christian living from friends, parents, teachers, and prayer.
Conclusion: We all need a shot sometimes. Make sure you get one when you need it.

This shot thing is called a syringe. We all know about getting shots. It's something that the doctor or nurse must do to help us get healthy or to stay healthy. It is more fun, however, to play with this than to get the real thing.

Why do we get shots? One kind of shot that we get is called an immunization. Immunizations protect us from getting serious illnesses such as polio, tetanus, measles, mumps, and diphtheria.

As Christians we need large shots of peace, joy, hope, and love to protect us from bad things that might infect our Christian lives. If we get these shots and boosters regularly, we will stay strong as Christians.

We get another kind of shot from the doctor when we are sick and need medicine to get better. The doctor puts medicine in the syringe. The medicine goes to work immediately because the nurse or doctor puts it right into our body.

Sometimes Christians get sick in their soul. Do you ever get sad or frustrated? We all do sometimes. When we get this way, we need a shot of encouragement. Let's say you are not getting along with your friend. You are always fighting over who gets what. You need a shot of sharing. What if you are jealous of your brother because he has been sick and is getting all the attention? You need a shot of love so you can feel sorry that he is sick and happy that people are trying to make him feel better. Suppose you are trying to make something and nothing is going right. You want to throw it across the room. You need a shot of patience so you can take a deep breath and keep working. Let's pretend that you took something. You would need a big shot of honesty so you could give it back and apologize. Did you ever think that because you were not getting your own way God didn't love you? You need a shot of faith. Have you ever felt really, really sad? You need a shot of hope.

Where do you get these shots? You don't need to go to the doctor. You can get them from friends. You can get them from parents and teachers. You can get them from praying. Sometimes you can get them from listening to the still, small voice of God inside you.

We all need a shot sometimes. Make sure you get one when you need it.

32

Fellowship

Object: glue stick, pieces of paper (or cutouts of simple people shapes) to represent members

Lesson: Fellowship means togetherness with God.

Outline

Introduce object: A glue stick is a handy thing to have.

1. The pieces of paper have equal value. Fellowship means everyone is equal in God's sight.
2. Fellowship means sticking together for a common purpose. God is the glue.
3. Gluing is more fun with more papers. Fellowship is the sharing of many.

Conclusion: Let's all love God together.

A glue stick is a handy thing to have. I'm always needing to stick things together. Today this glue stick is a handy thing to help me tell you about fellowship.

These pieces of paper have equal value. Fellowship means that everyone has the same value. A fellow is an equal. We are all equal in God's sight. Not one of us is more important than another. Our group needs you as much as it needs anyone else.

Let's stick these pieces of paper together. Fellowship means sticking together for a purpose. What is our purpose? We have come to worship God, to pray and to sing and to talk about him. What is our glue? God is the glue that sticks us together. If we didn't have this common purpose of worshiping God, we might begin to go in all different directions. Everyone might start to do whatever he or she wants to do, rather than what is good for God's group.

Can you have much fun with a glue stick if you have only one little piece of paper? You might fold it and glue it shut, but you can't do that very often. It is much better to have a whole bunch of pieces. So too we can't really fellowship by ourselves. Fellowship is sharing. We need other people. Fellowship is sharing ideas. Fellowship is telling problems and joys. Fellowship is praying together. Fellowship is singing the same song.

Being equals, sticking together to worship, and sharing all add up to togetherness with God. Let's all love God together.

33

Following Your Conscience

Object: the toy stethoscope from a child's medical kit
Lesson: We must listen to our conscience and keep it
  healthy.

Outline

Introduce object: There is a big name for this object.
1. Listen to your conscience, the still, small voice that
   speaks inside you, and follow it.
2. Your conscience should be clear like your lungs.
3. If your heart or lungs are sick, fix them. If your conscience is sick, fix it.
Conclusion: Keep a healthy conscience and let it guide you.

There is a big name for this object. It is called a stethoscope. Does anyone know what you do with it? The doctor uses it to listen to your heart. Your heart should sound
like this: "lub-dub." He also listens to your chest to hear
if your lungs are clear. He tells you to breathe deeply, and
he does not want to hear whooshing or gurgling when
you do.

When Christians talk about listening to our heart, they
mean the still, small voice inside of us that we call our
conscience. God gives us our conscience to help us know
what is right. If you are planning to take someone's toy
and a voice inside you tells you that would be stealing,
that voice is your conscience. Listen to it. If you hurt someone's feelings and you know it was wrong, that is your

conscience telling you. If you swear and a voice inside you says that is a bad thing to do, that is your conscience telling you. If you have a good conscience and follow it, you will be happy.

The doctor also wants you to have clear lungs. We talk about a clear conscience. Do you know what it means to have a clear conscience? It means that we have not done anything that we need to feel sorry for, or if we have, we have apologized. Do you have a clear conscience? Might there be a little, nagging secret back in the corner of it?

If the doctor hears something wrong in your heart or lungs, what will he do about it? He will test some more and maybe decide that you need an operation to make your heart right. If you have something in your conscience that is causing a problem, you need to operate on it. You need to get rid of it by making it right. If you have done something wrong, fix it. If you took something, give it back or replace it with a new one. If you lied, apologize. If you were unkind, begin to be kind.

Sometimes the doctor will give you medicine for gurgly lungs or a sick heart. What is the medicine for a sick conscience? It is a good dose of honesty, learning what is the right thing to do, and promising to do it. When your conscience is well again it can tell you what to do.

Keep a healthy conscience and let it guide you.

34

Forgiveness

Object: an erasable pen (or pencil)
Lesson: God wants us to forgive and forget.

Outline

Introduce object: I'm writing a note with this pen.
1. Everyone makes mistakes. That's why people make erasable pens.
2. God wants us to forgive, to erase the mistake.
3. God also wants us to forget, to write over the empty space.

Conclusion: Forgive as God forgave you.

I am writing a note with this pen. What if I make a mistake? I'll be okay because this is an erasable pen. Do you have erasable pens? I don't have to be afraid to make a mistake because I can erase it and try again.

Today I want to talk about forgiveness. Do any of you ever make mistakes with your friends or your family? Of course you do. You might even make a mistake and bump into a complete stranger. Everyone makes mistakes. You can't live your life always being afraid that you will make a mistake. God made apologies to take care of mistakes.

When you say or do something wrong, what do you do? You apologize. You expect the person you hurt to say, "That's okay" or "Don't worry about it" or "I forgive you." If you do something big like break your mother's favorite dish, you need a bigger apology, such as "I'm really sorry.

I promise to be more careful." If you hurt a friend's feelings, you say, "What can I do to make it up to you?" If you do something wrong on purpose, such as taking what doesn't belong to you, you need to apologize and make the wrong right by giving the thing back or replacing it.

If you or your feelings are hurt by another person, what will you do when he says he's sorry? God wants you to forgive him. You forgive him because he has apologized and needs to be forgiven. You also forgive him for yourself so that you will not become more and more angry and frustrated about what happened. This anger can make you sick. You should forgive the person.

Forgiving also means you will forget what happened. When I erase the mistake, you can hardly see it anymore. When I write what I wanted to say on top of what I erased, you can't tell the mistake was there at all. The mistake is completely gone. When you forgive a mistake or even something that was done on purpose, you need to forget about it completely and write over the place with new things about that person. If a friend took your toy but then gave it back and apologized, you must go on playing again like the friends you were. If a friend called you a name but apologized, you must go on talking and saying new, nicer things.

God wants us to forgive and forget. Forgive as God forgave you.

35

Friendship

Object: stuffed animals or dolls that hug (usually with Velcro on the hands)

Lesson: Friendship means caring for and about another person.

Outline

Introduce object: These little hugging monkeys have been in our family for a long time.
1. Friendship is a feeling.
2. Friendship is a way of acting.
3. Friendship means putting your friend first.
4. Friendship means not holding on too tightly.

Conclusion: It is wonderful to have special friends.

These little hugging monkeys have been in our family for a long time. I have always liked them because they remind me of friendship.

Friendship means that you have strong feelings for another person. You love that person. You enjoy being with him or her. You want to share your thoughts and feelings with that person. You trust him or her with your secrets. You have fun being together. These two monkeys are always together.

Friendship shows in your actions. You care about what happens to your friend. You want to share your toys with your friend. You want to help your friend whenever you can. When your friend is sad or upset, you will comfort him. These two monkeys are always hugging.

Friendship also means that you think about your friend first. You will be quick to forgive your friend. You will be patient when you need to wait for your friend. You will give her time to do what she needs to do. You don't need to have everything that your friend has; you can be happy for her when she gets something nice.

Friendship is not holding on so tightly that your friend does not have enough room to grow and live his own life. What are you saying, little monkey *[hold monkeys near your ear]?* Oh, your friend is holding you so tightly that you can't breathe? We'd better take these arms off for a minute. Now you have room to be yourself so that you can be better friends. Let me put you back together a little less tightly. I like seeing you together.

Friendship means caring for and about another person. It is wonderful to have special friends.

36

Goals

Object: toy cars, a car track
Lesson: Goals give direction to our lives as Christians.

Outline

Introduce object: How many of you have a track on which to speed your little cars?
1. You need a goal to aim toward. (Give examples.)
2. Don't jump the track and wind up going nowhere.
3. Don't slow down and stop before you reach your goal.
Conclusion: What goals do you have for your life?

How many of you have a track on which to speed your little cars? This one has several sections that can be attached to make a long track. If we can put one end up on a chair, the cars will pick up speed and run way into the other room. This track reminds me of goals. A goal is something you want out of life. If you want something or want to get somewhere, you need to go for that goal. If I set the far end of this track on the goal I want to reach, I can send this car right toward the goal. We all need something to aim for, otherwise we just wander around and don't know where we're going. Our parents can get us going in the right direction, but it's up to us to stay on track.

Let's think of some goals we might have for our lives. Why do you go to school? If you go to school to learn, you will learn. If you go there just because someone makes you, you will learn as little as possible and be very bored. Does God want you to use your mind and learn? Then make learning your goal.

If you and your group make a trip to a nursing home, your goal might be to make the old, sick people there happy. When you know this is your goal, you will do little things to make them smile, talk to them so they will not be lonely, sing for them so they can enjoy you, and let them sing along so they will have fun. If you do not have a goal in going there, you might just sit around and be miserable looking at the people.

When you send a car down this track, you want to be careful not to push it too hard. It might jump the track, and then it cannot go anywhere. So too, you don't want to be so impatient about reaching your goal that you jump the track and wind up going nowhere. If your goal is to make something for a friend to cheer him or her up, you don't want to rush so much that it gets broken or looks funny or falls apart.

When the car runs along this track, you do not want it to run out of steam and stop before it reaches the end. Sometimes the wheels of the car stick a little and the car goes for a while and then stops. It's easy to get stuck on the track to your goal by being discouraged or giving up or getting tired. Then you'll never reach it. My goal is to bring cheer to people around me. I don't want to run out of love or patience before I reach my goal.

Goals give direction to our lives as Christians. What goals do you have for your life?

37

Helpfulness

Object: the reflex hammer from a child's medical kit
Lesson: We need to help people.

Outline

Introduce object: (Hold up tool and describe.)

1. There's no reflex. Do you see when someone needs help?
2. There's an uncertain reflex. Will you help or turn away?
3. There's the speed of the reflex. How soon will you help?

Conclusion: How quickly do you react to help someone?

Here is an instrument from a doctor's kit. It is used to tap the patient just below the knee to find out about his or her reflex. A good reflex is a quick kick. Have you ever tried to use one of these?

When the doctor taps your knee with this hammer, he hopes to find that you have a good reflex. If you don't kick, he or she will try again. If you don't respond at all, the doctor will need to do more tests.

Today I am talking about another kind of reflex: the re-action to someone needing help. This helping reflex has to come from your mind and your heart. People who have no helping reflex are so concerned with themselves that they don't even see when someone else needs help. That's pretty selfish. It is also not healthy. God didn't put you on this earth full of people to think only of yourself. People who spend all their time and energy saying, "What about me?" "That's mine!" "Give me that!" are not happy. This is not the kind of person Jesus wants you to be.

Sometimes when a doctor tests your reflexes, the reflexes are there, but they aren't working right. Some people's helping reflexes don't work right. They are not sure what to do when they see someone in need of help. They may turn away. Would this be a helpful reflex? When you see someone crying, do you turn away, or do you offer to help? When you see that someone is hungry, do you give him some of your food? If you know someone is lonely, will you spend time with her? If a friend is sick, will you ask to visit? If there is a mess, will you help pick it up? If friends are sad, will you try to cheer them up? Or will you pretend that none of these situations are happening?

Another thing that concerns the doctor is how quickly you react. Your leg should jerk out right away. If it takes you too long to react, that's not a good sign. That is true of helping as well. When a person needs help, he needs it now, not whenever you feel like getting around to giving it. If I were carrying a bunch of things and couldn't get the door open, I couldn't stand around waiting for you to finish what you were doing. If someone is crying, you wouldn't wait to help her until she has stopped.

Keep your eyes open. There are chances to help people all around you. When you help others, it makes you feel good inside. How quickly do you react to help someone?

38

Positive Thinking

Object: toy bandages from a child's medical kit
Lesson: We can protect ourselves by thinking about things that are good.

Outline

Introduce object: Is there anyone here who has never needed a bandage?
1. What are some bad germs that can cause an infection in our hearts and minds? (hatred, jealousy, lying)
2. How do we keep them out? By covering ourselves with positive things. (love, gratitude, honesty)
Conclusion: Protect yourself with good thoughts.

Is there anyone here who has never needed a bandage? We all need one at one time or another. Why? What does a bandage do? It protects our cuts and sores. First you clean out a cut. You might need to apply pressure to get it to stop bleeding. Then you put on a bandage to keep the germs out. It is important to keep the germs out so your cut does not become infected.

When the Bible tells us to think about things that are good and honest and beautiful, it is telling us to keep out the bad germs that might infect us. Let's think of some bad germs that might get inside our minds and hearts. How about hating? If you hate someone, you dislike her so much that you are mean to her. If you hate someone, you feel mean inside. This meanness can infect you so that you become mean to other people, and you feel miserable. Jealousy is another bad germ. If you are jealous of your friend, you want what he has. You become infected with wanting, and you do not appreciate what you have. You become unhappy. Lying is another bad germ. One lie leads to another until you have an infection of lies.

How do you keep these and other bad germs out? What kind of bandage can you put on your heart? The Bible tells us to keep a bandage of pure, clean thoughts on our hearts. If we cover our hearts with good thoughts, it will be very hard for the bad germs to get in. If you love people with Jesus' love, it will be hard to begin to hate. You will forgive someone long before you can get to hating her. If you thank God for your blessings and enjoy all the wonderful things he has given you, you won't have time for jealousy. If you value truth and are honest, the lies won't creep in.

Keep the germs out of your heart and mind. Protect yourself with good thoughts.

39

Reading the Bible

Object: an unfamiliar game with directions how to play
Lesson: The Bible is your book of directions.

Outline

Introduce object: This looks like an interesting game.
1. Without the directions the game is pointless. Christians have the Bible for their directions.
2. The directions give us rules for playing the game fairly. The Bible contains rules for living.
3. The directions give us information for more enjoyment of the game. The Bible helps us live happier lives.

Conclusion: If you can't read the Bible, have someone read it to you.

This looks like an interesting game. I have never played it before. How should we go about playing it? We could take out these pieces and look at the game board and think up some things to do. If we try to do it this way, we might not have a very interesting game. I think we would run out of things to do and grow tired of playing the game. Can you think of a better way?

We could read the directions. That would tell us what to do. There are directions here on the box that tell us the best way to play the game.

There is a set of directions for Christian living also. In fact, there is a whole book of stories and poems and letters, all giving us information on how to live the Christian life. Do you know what that book is called? It is the Bible. Doesn't it make sense for us to read the directions to our lives?

The directions for this game will give us rules for playing the game fairly. They include things such as taking turns and gaining points. There are things we need to know about living the Christian life also. We need to know what God expects from us. We need to know more about God and how he runs his world.

The directions to this game also tell us some other things we can do to make the game even more fun. The same is true of the Bible. It tells us of the wonderful things that Jesus did so we can love him even more. It gives us ideas to live a happier life. It helps us sing and pray and worship. It tells us interesting stories.

The Bible is your book of directions. If you can't read the Bible, have someone read it to you.

40

Resolving Conflict

Object: two action figures
Lesson: God wants us to solve our conflicts peacefully.

Outline

Introduce object: These two action figures were created to be solving problems.
1. TV is not real life.
2. God wants our action to be with our minds and mouths.
3. Turn the other cheek.
Conclusion: Are you willing to do the tough thing?

These two action figures were created to be jumping out of trouble, saving the person in distress from danger, and solving the problems of the world.

Unfortunately, we often see figures like this on TV doing a lot of fighting. The reason they fight on TV is because the people who made the show want you to watch the program to see who wins the fight. They think you will lose interest if the characters talk about their problems or sit and think of ways to solve the mystery and catch the bad person.

The problem with TV programs like this is that when children play with the action figures, the children make the toys fight each other because the children think fighting is how problems are really solved. Think for yourself. Do things get better or worse when you hit and punch and kick another person? They get worse. Hitting just causes another problem to deal with.

God wants his action figures to take action by doing something better than slugging it out. God wants us to think about what is happening. What is the problem? How did it start? What can be done to solve it? Let's say you and your friend are fighting about whose turn it is to ride a bicycle. There are several ways to solve the problem. Hitting is not one of them. You could try to get another bicycle and ride together. You might try riding around the block or a set distance so that the turns are equal. If you have a watch, you could time the turns. If you can't decide whose turn it is, one person will have to be better and let the other go first. You might decide to do something else altogether. By working on it, you have solved your problem and perhaps even become better friends.

In the Bible, we are told that if someone hits us we should "turn the other cheek." That means even if the other person started a fight, we should not fight back. We have to say, "I would like to hit you back, but I am not going to. I don't want to hurt you. If you won't talk about the problem, I am going to leave." Now, the one who says those words is the smartest and the strongest person. Saying such words is hard to do! But God wants us to solve our problems peacefully. Are you willing to do the tough thing?

41

Responsibility

Object: a set of blocks or Legos, container that holds them

Lesson: Responsibility is doing what you should without being told.

Outline

Introduce object: I have a big container filled with blocks.
1. A responsible person keeps his or her promises.
2. A responsible person does what is right.
3. A responsible person will help when needed.
4. A responsible person makes good choices.

Conclusion: Are you a responsible person?

I have a big container filled with blocks. Would you like me to dump them out so we can play with them? Will you help me pick them up?

Today we are talking about responsibility. It is a long word that means doing what you should be doing without having to be told. If you said that you would help pick up the blocks, you should do it. A responsible person keeps his or her promises.

If you didn't promise to pick up the blocks, but you did play with them, should you still pick them up? Yes, a responsible person does what is right. If you played with them, you should help pick them up.

What if everyone started to leave, and you saw me all alone here picking up all of these blocks—would you come back and help? A responsible person will offer help when it is needed. A responsible person would see that it was not fair for me to be picking up all the blocks alone.

Many times we find we need to make choices. When you make good choices, you are being responsible. When you put down your own answers on a test, you are being responsible. When you take good care of a borrowed toy or tool, you are being responsible. When you find matches and give them quickly to an adult, you are being responsible. When you look carefully before you cross a street (or stay in the yard if you are not allowed to cross the street), you are being responsible. When people can depend on you, you are being responsible.

God wants us to be responsible people. Are you a responsible person?

42

Singing God's Praises

Object: a child's sing-along tape and tape player
Lesson: We sing to praise God.

Outline

Introduce object: This is a sing-along tape.
1. We sing because it is fun.
2. We sing because there are wonderful songs that we can sing to praise God.
3. We sing because God loves to hear his children singing songs about him.
Conclusion: I like to think that God smiles when he hears his children singing.

This is a sing-along tape. Let me play a little of it for you. It has *Sesame Street* songs on it that I think you might know.

Why do we have sing-along tapes and videos? Many times it is more fun to sing with other people than to sing alone. That's why we sing together here: It is fun to sing and praise God together. Singing along with others also helps us sing better. It keeps us on pitch and up to tempo. The instruments also help us. In Bible times people used many kinds of instruments. I like using different instruments too. Sometimes one person sings and the rest of us listen. Often we sing whether or not anyone is listening. Any way, singing is fun.

There are some cute, happy songs on the tape. We sing about lots of things when we sing with this tape. Do you ever wonder what we are singing about in church? There are some wonderful messages in children's songs: "Jesus loves me, this I know for the Bible tells me so" and "Jesus loves the little children, all the children of the world" and "Hallelujah, praise the Lord." Let's take a closer look at some of your favorites *[ask for song titles and, if time permits, discuss each one]*. Do you mean the words you sing when you sing God's praises? We sing because of those words.

Another very important reason we sing and praise God is because God loves to hear his children singing. All throughout Bible times and through to today, people have been singing God's praises, singing about how wonderful God is. God enjoys our singing just as we enjoy singing to him.

We sing to praise God. I like to think that God smiles when he hears his children singing.

43

Talking Wisely

Object: a talking toy or a tape recorder

Lesson: God wants us to think before we speak and to consider the consequences of our spoken words.

Outline

Introduce object: This toy talks.
1. Some people talk without thinking.
2. Some people talk unkindly on purpose.
3. You can talk wisely.

Conclusion: Do you talk wisely?

This toy talks. When I talk into this microphone, the doll says the same thing that I do. Actually, I'm doing the talking. Her mouth is just moving. This toy will help me talk about talking or, in some cases, not talking.

This doll says everything I say. Some people say everything that comes to their mind without thinking. They may say, "That shirt looks stupid." Someone's feelings could be hurt. Saying to someone, "Your brother is a jerk" could make that person angry. Saying to a person, "Someone is out to get you" could make that person feel scared. Saying whatever comes to mind can be a dangerous thing to do. You can get hurt or another person can get hurt. Sometimes you need to keep your mouth still. You can learn a lot by keeping your mouth shut and your ears open.

This doll has to say whatever I say. She can't think for herself. Often people who can think for themselves still don't think about what they say, or they say unkind things on purpose. Do you think God wants us to do this? Listen to the doll: "You have a fat neck. That looks really dumb. Your father doesn't have a job. Why do you always wear those old clothes? Your car is a piece of junk. My bike is nicer than yours. Can't you get a better house?" Teasing and taunting are cruel. You are smart enough to know that some things should not be said.

Sometimes even the truth is said in the wrong way. Which is better, saying, "You stink" or "Let's go for a swim"? How about, "That dress is old and funny looking" or "You can wear one of my dresses"? When you think first, you can find a way to speak the truth in love. You can also say things that make people feel better, such as "You are looking happy today," "I like your shoes," "That was a funny story." Telling the truth in a kind way and saying things to make people feel good about themselves are examples of talking wisely.

God made you so you could talk. He wants you to think before you speak. Do you talk wisely?

44

Trusting God

Object: a big stick

Lesson: God helps and protects his people.

Outline

Introduce object: I found this big stick in our garage.
1. A big stick can keep you from falling. So can God.
2. A big stick can ward off danger. God will protect you.
3. A big stick can help you reach high places. God will too.
4. You can grab a big stick and be pulled to safety. God keeps us safe.

Conclusion: God is like a powerfully big stick. You can lean on him for help.

I found this big stick in our garage. I think it was left there a few years ago by our son, Peter. He was always using big sticks for one thing or another. I can think of several uses for this big stick.

People often carry a big stick when they go for a walk, especially if they walk in uneven, slippery, or rocky places. Let's think of God as our big stick. Whenever we go to new or strange places, he will be our stick to hold us up and keep us from falling. There are many times when I have to hold tightly onto God to keep from chickening out, doing the wrong thing, or saying unkind words.

People also use a big stick to ward off danger. If a big dog is coming after you, you can wave a big stick and scare it away. A big stick makes you feel safer. It makes me feel safer knowing that God is always with me to protect me. He won't let anything happen to me.

I would also use a big stick if I couldn't quite reach something. I would use a big stick with a cloth on it to reach a spot on the ceiling. I would use a big stick to knock a can off a very high shelf. We can reach more happiness with God's help.

Another way to use a big stick is to help someone. One time I was having trouble swimming. A friend held a big stick out to me, and I grabbed onto it and was pulled to the shore. You could be slipping down the side of a hill, and someone could hold out a big stick for you to grab. We can hold onto our faith in God and trust him to help us when we are in trouble. He will save us. God is like a powerfully big stick. You can lean on him for help.

45

Walking Wisely

Object: a walking toy
Lesson: Be careful, little feet, where you go.

Outline

Introduce object: This little wind-up toy can walk.
1. God wants us to walk, move about, and make choices.
2. We need to pay attention to where we are going.
3. There are many places we can and should go.
Conclusion: Are you careful about where your feet take you?

This little wind-up toy can walk. When I turn the key on the back, it can go on its own. Watch out! It is walking right off the table.

Can you walk on your own? Of course you can. God made you so that you could walk around by yourself. He wants you to be able to make choices and go places. He gave you your feet. It is great to be able to move about on your own. Just ask anyone who has had an accident and cannot walk.

Can you go anywhere you want? This wind-up toy walks anywhere it wants. In fact, it would walk right off the table. God gave you a brain so that even though you can go anywhere you want, you might not choose to. Let's think of some places we should not go: into someone's house when we are not invited, into the car of a stranger, out of a store without paying for what we have gotten there, to bad movies, into unsafe neighborhoods. Can you think of more?

Are there places you should be going? There are good places that our feet should be taking us. There are kind and productive things that we should be doing. God wants us to walk into church, to walk into school, to walk into the store for our mother, to walk into a friend's or relative's house and give him or her a hug, and to walk into appropriate plays and programs. Can you think of more places our feet should be taking us?

Do you remember the song that says, "Oh, be careful, little feet, where you go"? That song means that we should be very careful where we let our feet take us. We want to go only in the places that would be good for us. Are you careful about where your feet take you?

46

Witnessing

Object: the doctor's bag that comes with a child's medical kit

Lesson: What we say and do reflects our Christianity.

Outline

Introduce object: When you see a person carrying a bag like this, what do you think about that person?

1. You can tell a doctor or a Christian from the outside.
2. It is important for people to see that Christians have something special inside.
3. In a doctor's bag are the necessary tools. In a Christian's heart are the necessary tools.

Conclusion: What tools do you carry in your heart?

When you see a person carrying a bag like this, what do you think about that person? Yes, you think the person is a doctor who has come to make someone better. You know that a doctor carries with him the medicine and equipment he needs to treat people when he goes out to work. You can get a good idea about who he is just by looking at the outside.

Is there any way people can tell who are Christians by the outside? I certainly hope so. You can see if they go to church on Sunday. You can see if they read the Bible or other books about God. You can see if they act kindly toward others. You can see if they smile frequently because they have a special love inside. You can certainly tell by the things they say and the language they use.

Should you know from the outside who is a doctor? If there is an accident and a person comes to help, I would like to see that it is a doctor who has the medicine and equipment to help. If I am waiting for a doctor, I will be relieved to see a person with a doctor's bag coming. I will know help is near.

Should people be able to see from the outside that you are a Christian? This is even more important. If Christ is in your heart, you should be different. People should see you have a certain quality of love and patience like an inner glow that shines through what you do.

Why is this important? It is necessary for you to live the way you believe. You won't feel well if you think one way and act another. It is important for people to see that we have something special inside so they will want to know and love Jesus too. It is necessary for other Christians to act toward each other the way Jesus would want them to act because this pleases Jesus.

In a doctor's bag are the tools he needs to be a doctor. You wouldn't expect to find his dirty laundry in there. In a Christian's heart are the tools needed for a happy Christian life. You would expect to find the right things in there also. What tools do you carry in your heart?

47
Worship

Object: a group game such as one played at a birthday party (Mother, May I; Simon Says; Pin the Tail; etc.)

Lesson: Worship is an act of loving God with our body, mind, and heart.

Outline

Introduce object: (Describe how to play the game. Play it if time and room permit.)

1. To play the game, you use your body. To worship, you use your body to sing, pray, and read.
2. To play the game, you need to be thinking. To worship, you need to pay attention.
3. To play the game successfully, you need to have your heart in it. To truly worship, your heart must love God and want to praise him.

Conclusion: Are all your parts worshiping God today?

Today we are going to play a game called Mother, May I. Everyone line up. I will tell you to take a certain number of big, medium, or baby steps. Before you can take them, you must remember to say, "Mother, may I?" If you take the steps without saying this, you have to go back to the starting line and begin all over again. The first ones to reach that point over there are the winners.

The reason I explained this game is because it will help me tell you about worship. Worship is an act of loving God. We can love him by thinking about him, singing and praying to him, and reading and talking about him.

We worship by each taking our own steps. Just as everyone moved his or her own body in the game, so everyone uses his or her own body in singing or praying or reading the Bible.

In order to play the game, you needed to be paying attention with your mind. If you just let your body play the game, you would move without thinking to ask, "Mother, may I?" In order to worship, you need to be paying attention. If you are just sitting there thinking about something completely different, you are not worshiping. You need to listen and think.

To do well in the game we played, you needed to want to play it. If your heart was not in it, you would take very small steps and not get very far. In order to worship, your heart must be in it. Your heart must love God and want to praise him. Then your heart will be happy because everyone is loving God together. Worship should give you a warm feeling inside.

Many times you worship alone with God. Here we worship and love God together.

Worship is loving God with your body, mind, and heart. Are all your parts worshiping God today?

48

All in the Family

Object: a toy family (pieces from a dollhouse, Playskool sets, etc.)

Lesson: There are many kinds of Christian families.

Outline

Introduce object: Crissy brought the little people from her dollhouse today.

1. Families may have a mother and father and any number of children. If they love and serve God together, they are a Christian family.
2. Families who adopt or don't have children are still Christian families if they love and serve God together.
3. Combined families are Christian families if they love and serve God together.

Conclusion: What makes a family a Christian family is that they love and serve God together.

Crissy brought the little people from her dollhouse today. These family pieces can help me talk about the Christian family.

The Christian family starts by God bringing two people together who love each other. Here are the woman and man getting married and promising to love each other and to be faithful and kind to one another forever. They promise this in front of God and the friends and family who come to the wedding.

After they are married, God blesses them with cute little babies like you all were. There may be more and more babies. There is no set number of people in a Christian family. There may be a mother and father and one or many children. What makes them a Christian family is that they love God and pray and go to church and read the Bible together. They have problems, but they work them out.

Sometimes the mother and father cannot have babies. There might be something physically wrong with either the father or the mother. These people might adopt a baby. They are a Christian family because they love God and are very thankful to him for the child they can adopt.

Sometimes two people who are married decide for whatever reason that they will not have any children. Two people are still a Christian family if they love God together.

Sometimes one of the parents in a family dies or breaks his or her wedding promise and leaves. This is sad, but there is still a Christian family if the ones left love God together. God will give them extra help because there is only one parent.

There are times when a mother having to raise children by herself meets a man who may or may not have children. They combine to make a bigger family. It is a challenge for everybody to get along, but they are still a Christian family if they sing and pray and love God together.

A family is any number of people that God puts together to eat and sleep and take care of each other. It may include grandparents, uncles and aunts, or even friends. What makes a family a Christian family is that they love and serve God together.

Racial Diversity

Object: a big box of crayons and a piece of paper
Lesson: God made people of all colors and characteristics.

Outline

Introduce object: I love a big box of crayons.
1. God made his world different colors so it would be more beautiful.
2. God made people different colors so the world would be more interesting.
3. One color is not better than another, in flowers or people.

Conclusion: God loves all colors of people. He made them the way they are. We should love them too.

I love a big box of crayons. Do you like to draw? I can draw flowers. Let me make some. These are supposed to be red tulips and pink roses and yellow daisies and purple violets and golden marigolds and orange azaleas and lots of green leaves *[picture may already be drawn]*.

Would this picture look as nice if I had only used one or two colors? God didn't make his world one or two colors. He made it many colors so that it would be beautiful. That's why we need a big box of different-colored crayons to draw it. God made a big, beautiful, wonderful world.

If I put a person in this picture, what color should I use for the skin? White wouldn't look good. Nobody is truly white unless she puts powder or white makeup all over her skin. Even people we call white are any shade from deep tan to pale peach. Like the flowers, God gave his people different colors. He wanted to make his world more interesting. He gave people colors of skin that fit them best.

Wouldn't it be strange if one flower said, "I am better because I am purple and everybody knows that purple is a royal color." I wonder why some people think that one color of skin is better than another. What makes a person good or bad? Is it the color of his skin? What makes one person friendly and another mean? Is it the color of their skin? What makes one person give freely and another steal? Is it the color of their skin? No, it is what is in the heart of the person. The difference is on the inside.

When God hears a prayer, do you think he cares about the color of the person praying? When someone dies and goes to heaven, do you think God cares about that person's color? God loves all colors of people. He made them the way they are. We should love them too.

50
Equality

Object: a nesting or stacking toy
Lesson: Each person is important in God's sight.

Outline

Introduce object: (Describe your set.)
1. If one piece is missing, the set is incomplete. If you were not here, we would miss you.
2. It doesn't matter which one is missing. God made us all equal.
3. All the dolls fit together snugly and perfectly. We all fit together in fellowship.

Conclusion: God made each one of us. Each one of us is important.

We brought this set of seven nesting dolls back from our trip to Russia. They all have the same pear shape, but each one is slightly larger than the one before it. They all open up, except the smallest one. The smallest one fits into the one a little bit larger, and that one fits into the next one, and so on. These dolls are painted to look like Russian leaders from the past. This is also an adult toy.

When all of the dolls in this set are lined up, you can see how each one is important. They make a neat set. What if one of these dolls were missing? Our set would not be complete. You would be able to tell right away that one was missing. They wouldn't line up evenly. When you would try to put them back inside each other, it would be harder to tell which one should come next. Each person who is here today is important. God made you. God loves you. We want you here. You make us complete. If you weren't here, we'd miss you.

Once, the smallest doll of this set was missing. It is the one that doesn't open up. We looked all over the house for it because our set was ruined without this piece. If one piece is missing from this set, it doesn't make a difference which one is gone. Any one of them would be missed. Each of them is just as important as any other. So too, each one of you is just as important as another. It doesn't make any difference if you are the smallest. It doesn't make any difference if you don't open up much. Each person is just as important as any other person here. God made us all equally wonderful.

All of these dolls are different, but they're made to be a set. They fit together snugly and perfectly. We may look different, but we are all made by God. He made us part of a set. We fit together in fellowship. God made each one of us. Each one of us is important.

51

God's Beautiful World

Object: a kaleidoscope
Lesson: God gave us an incredibly beautiful world.

Outline

Introduce object: Do you know what this is called?

1. The kaleidoscope has sparkling colors because it is made with bright pieces of colored glass and mirrors. God made the earth with beautiful colors.
2. Each turn of the kaleidoscope shows us something new. Each season brings something new and wonderful.
3. No two pictures are exactly the same. No two snowflakes, etc., are exactly the same.
4. A kaleidoscope is a thing of wonder. The world is a wonderful place.

Conclusion: I thank God for this big, beautiful world.

Do you know what this is called? It has a long name: kaleidoscope. The parts of this word mean *beautiful* and *form*. The earth that God made for us to live on also has beautiful form.

The kaleidoscope has sparkling colors because it is made with small pieces of brightly colored glass that are reflected by mirrors in this tube. God's earth has wonderful colors because God made it that way. It has different shades of blue and white and gray in the sky, various greens in the grass and trees, all colors imaginable in the flowers, and many browns in the dirt.

The colors in the kaleidoscope change as you turn the tube. The little pieces of glass fall and are reflected differently by the mirrors. So too the colors around us change. Spring brings brighter greens and lots of flowers. Summer has growing vegetables and fruits, inviting lakes, and interesting skies. The fall, which is my favorite time of year, has the most marvelous colors in the trees and bushes. I also love a soft, fresh, white coat of snow on the trees and lawns in winter.

No two pictures in the kaleidoscope are exactly the same because the little pieces of glass fall differently as the tube is turned. You can't make them fall in the same way. The colors of the world are always different too. No two sunsets are exactly the same. Each snowflake is different from the others. Each tree is shaped in its own way as it grows. Every mountain has its own character.

The kaleidoscope is a thing of wonder and beauty. This is a wonderful, beautiful world. Each day we can enjoy what God has given us as we look around us. When we look farther away, we see even more. I love traveling to other places, even other countries, to see this world that God has made. I thank God for this big, beautiful world.

52

Saying No

Object: a much valued, breakable toy
Lesson: Say no to things that are harmful.

Outline

Introduce object: Megan brought her favorite toy for us to see.
1. Say no to drugs, including cigarettes.
2. Say no to going with strangers.
3. Say no to people touching you in a way that makes you feel uncomfortable.
Conclusion: Will you take good care of your body?

Megan brought her favorite toy for us to see. I know she really likes this toy. It is a china figure of a lion. She has wrapped it very carefully so it won't break. Would this break if I dropped it on the floor? Yes, it would. Megan, if I asked you to throw this china lion against the wall, would you do it? No, you wouldn't because it would be wrong. There are other things that happen to us that are wrong. God wants you to say no to those things.

If anyone, big person or little person, tried to get you to take drugs or to smoke a cigarette, what would you say? Saying that you will try it makes as much sense as taking something you value and breaking it. It is, in fact, taking the body that you will need to live in for many, many years and risking its health. If anyone ever asks you to smoke or take drugs, think of taking your body—like a favorite, breakable toy—and smashing it against the wall.

What if a stranger tries to get you to go with him or her? Remember, a stranger will offer you candy or say that your mother wants you or try to get you to help him or her somehow. A good stranger will know you are doing the right thing by running away. A bad stranger will try even harder to get you. Tell the stranger that you will go and get help, and leave right away. Going with a stranger is like taking your most valuable thing, your body, and smashing it.

Another problem that you may face is having someone, even an adult whom you know, touch you in a way that makes you feel uncomfortable. Children think such touching must be okay because a big person did it. Children think big people know what is right. But is it true that big people never do anything wrong? No, anybody can do bad things. Growing up doesn't make people good. If a person—no matter who it is—touches you in places that you don't want to be touched, tell somebody.

Megan is going to take good care of her favorite toy. Will you take good care of your body?